Inside SPORT

CRICKET

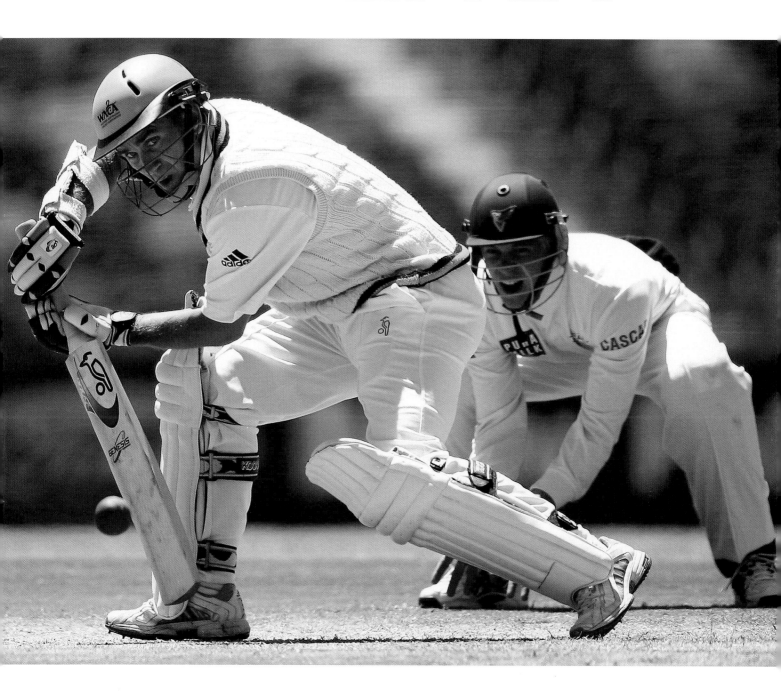

Clive Gifford

WAYLAND

First published in 2008 by Wayland

Copyright © Wayland 2008

Wayland
338 Euston Road
London NW1 3BH

Wayland Australia
Level 17/207 Kent Street
Sydney NSW 2000

Senior Editor: Jennifer Schofield
Designer: Rachel Hamdi and Holly Fulbrook
Illustrator: Ian Thompson and Holly Fulbrook
Picture Researcher: Clive Gifford
Proofreader: Patience Coster

Picture Acknowledgements:
The author and publisher would like to thank the following agencies for allowing these
pictures to be reproduced: cover, 20 Adrian Dennis/AFP/Getty Images; 1, 8, 18, 43 Paul Kane/Getty
Images; 3, 35 Darren England/Getty Images; 4 Stu Forster/Getty Images; 5 Allessandro
Abbonizio/AFP/Getty Images; 6 Michael Steele/Getty Images; 7 Manan Vatsyayana/AFP/Getty Images; 9
Christophe Archambault/AFP/Getty Images; 10, 23 Greg Wood/AFP/Getty Images; 12 Alex Livesey/Getty
Images; 14 Phil Walter/Getty Images; 15, 46 Hachette Children's Books; 17 Stringer/AFP/Getty Images; 19
Gallo Images/Getty Images; 21, 36, 37 Saeed Khan/AFP/Getty Images; 22 Laurence Griffiths/Getty Images;
24 Nick Wilson/Getty Images; 25 Jewel Samad/AFP/Getty Images; 26, 28 Dean Treml/AFP/Getty Images; 27,
40 Hamish Blair/Getty Images; 29 Farjand K Godhuly/AFP/Getty Images; 30 Clive Rose/Getty Images; 31
Mark Nolan/Getty Images; 32 Laurence Griffiths/Getty Images; 33 Alexander Joe/AFP/Getty Images; 34
William West/AFP/Getty Images; 38 Deshakalyan Chowditury/AFP/Getty Images; 39 Richard
Heathcote/Getty; Images; 41 Evening Standard/Hulton Archive/Getty Images; 42 Ben Radford/Getty
Images; 44 Prakash Singh/AFP/Getty Images/ 45 Adrian Murrell/Getty Images

CIP data
    Gifford, Clive
    Cricket. - (Inside sport)
    1. Cricket - Juvenile literature
    I. Title
    796.3'58

ISBN: 978 0 7502 5250 8

Printed in China

Wayland is a division of Hachette Children's Books, an Hachette Livre UK company

CONTENTS

INTRODUCTION

Cricket is an epic battle of wits, skills and athleticism between two sides. It can seem a complicated game with its many laws, but the main aim of the game is simple – to score more runs than the opposing side by hitting the ball using a bat. The fielding side aims to stop runs and get the batsmen out.

World Appeal

Cricket began in England but has since spread all over the globe. Elite cricket is organized by the International Cricket Council (ICC), which was founded in 1909. Today the ICC has 97 member countries. Only ten teams play Test match cricket, the highest form of the game, but many more play in other competitions. For example at the 2007 ICC World Cup, Ireland pulled off the shock of the tournament by beating Pakistan. All over the world, passionate fans flock to watch games live while millions more follow the excitement on radio, television and the Internet.

Cricket is far from a gentle game. It is an athletic sport requiring high levels of fitness, stamina and concentration. Bowlers bowl a series of six balls, or deliveries, known as an over. They may bowl 25 or more overs a day and thousands of overs throughout their career. Batsmen have to concentrate for hours on end as the ball hurtles towards them at speeds of between 80 and 150km/h, while fielders have to be ready to swoop, sprint and dive to stop the ball.

Although cricket is an outdoor sport, different forms of the game are played indoors in sports halls, and by younger players learning the game. These include Kwik Cricket, which is known as Kanga Cricket in Australia and Kiwi Cricket in New Zealand. This is a fast and fun game played by any number of young players using a plastic bat, ball and stumps.

Kevin Pietersen pulls the ball to the boundary on his way to his first double-century in Test match cricket against the West Indies in 2007.

One Innings or Two

Each team's turn to bat is called an innings. All 11 players can have the chance to bat, two at a time. When one of the two batsmen is out, the next batsman in a team replaces him. In Test matches, a team's innings is over when ten of the 11 players are out. The other team usually then takes its turn to bat. In Test matches, both teams get two innings per match. In limited overs games, such as One Day Internationals (ODIs), each team bats once and the team's innings ends when either ten of its batsmen are out or the maximum number of overs has been bowled.

MAD FACT

Pakistan's Saqlain Mushtaq bowled an incredible 107.2 overs (644 balls) to Sri Lankan batsmen in a match in 1997.

Sri Lanka's Sanath Jayasuriya in action. Jayasuriya has scored over 12,000 ODI runs.

CRICKET THEN AND NOW

Cricket has a long history. The first match between English counties, for example, occurred when Kent played Surrey in 1709. In the 1860s, a revolutionary new rule was added, allowing overarm bowling. Up to this point, bowling had been gentle underarm lobs. This rule change, and many others over the years, paved the way for the absorbing contest between bat and ball that is called cricket today.

Marcus Trescothick throws himself to his left to catch a ball during fielding practice. Modern cricketers train and practise intensely to help hone their skills and fitness levels.

The Home of Cricket

In 1787, Thomas Lord formed a private cricket ground in London, England, and founded the Marylebone Cricket Club (MCC). The following year, the MCC published a set of Laws of Cricket that became adopted by clubs everywhere. The MCC moved its ground in 1814 to the present site, named Lords, which is now the most famous ground in the world.

Bat and Ball

Early cricket bats were curved hooks, ideal for scooping up the ball, but by the nineteenth century they were straight and carved out of willow wood. A cricket bat must be less than 96.5cm long and 10.8cm wide. The cricket ball is made from cork and wool, covered in a leather casing stitched together to form a raised seam. Balls are red for Test matches and many other competitions, but white for ODIs so that they show up better under floodlights and against the players' coloured clothing. In a Test match, the ball can become battered, and so after 80 overs the fielding team can decide if it wants to take a new ball supplied by the umpires. A new ball is harder and bounces more than an old one.

Protection and Padding

Since the 1830s, leg pads have been worn by batsmen, and from the 1850s, by wicketkeepers to protect their lower legs. Amazingly, protective helmets did not appear until the 1970s. Today's helmets for batsmen and some close fielders usually come with a metal grille or shatterproof plastic visor to protect the batsman's face. With the rock-hard cricket ball flying towards them at speeds of 140km/h or more, batsmen wear padding to protect other vulnerable areas, too. These include forearm and elbow protectors, padded batting gloves, a thigh pad worn on the leg closest to the bowler, and sometimes a chest protector. For male players, a box worn inside the trousers is also essential.

Professionals and Practice

Cricket was once seen as a game for wealthy gentlemen who rarely trained or practised. Some would even hire ordinary workers to do their bowling or fielding for them. Today, top players are professionals, paid to play the sport. They work hard on their fitness levels in the gym and out in cricket nets, honing their bowling actions and batting strokes. They also go through hours of fielding drills to sharpen their catching, ball gathering and throwing skills.

A ball gets stuck in the metal grille of Indian batsman, Gautam Gambhir's helmet. His padded batting gloves and combined forearm and elbow protector can be clearly seen. He is wearing typically colourful One Day International team clothing. For Test matches and many other matches, white trousers and shirts are worn.

AIM OF THE GAME

Cricket is an 11-a-side team game where one side bowls the ball and fields while the other team bats, defends its stumps and aims to score runs. A team can score one or more runs per delivery (each ball bowled) in a number of different ways.

The Stumps and Crease

At each end of the pitch is a row of three wooden stumps topped by two horizontal wooden cylinders, called bails. Together, the three stumps and the bails form a wicket. Surrounding each wicket is a collection of markings, known as creases. The line just in front of the stumps is called the bowling crease. The line 1.22m in front of the stumps and parallel with the bowling crease is the popping crease. This line must be crossed by the batsman's bat for a run to be scored.

Hitting Runs

The most common way of scoring runs is when the batsman hits the ball into a space and he and the other batsman run to each other's end. A run is scored once the batsmen have crossed and touched the ground past the popping crease with their bats. Batsmen can turn and complete another run providing they have grounded their bats behind the popping crease. If not, the umpire will signal a short run (by tapping his shoulder with his fingers) and the run will not count.

return creases mark the side edges of the crease area

stumps with bails on top

bowling crease

popping crease

Australian fast bowler, Brett Lee, has run up to the crease and is about to release the ball.

A strong stroke by a batsman may see the ball race past fielders and reach and touch or cross the edge of the field, known as the boundary. Six runs are awarded when the ball reaches the boundary without bouncing, and if the ball bounces but still reaches the boundary four runs are scored. Sometimes the fielding team leaves a helmet on the ground for close fielders. If the batsman's shot hits this helmet, the umpire awards five runs.

Extras

These are runs added to a team's total but not to the batsman's individual score. Byes are when a run is taken but the batsman did not hit the ball. Leg byes occur when the ball came off the batsman's pads or body while he was trying to play a shot or avoid being hit by the ball. The two other main forms of extras – wides and no-balls – are penalties imposed on a bowler (see page 16–17).

Pakistan batsmen Shahid Afridi (left) and Salman Butt cross over as they run during a 2005 ODI against India.

OUT!

A batsman continues to bat until either his team declares (see page 23), the innings ends in a limited overs game, he retires hurt or ill, or he is out, known as a dismissal. Whether a batsman is out or not is decided by the umpire after the fielding team appeals by asking: "How's that?".

Run-out!

The pressure to score quick runs can sometimes lead to risks being taken or miscommunication between the batsmen. Quick, accurate fielding can then lead to a run-out. Run-outs occur when the fielding side hits the stumps and knocks off the bails with the ball before the batsman grounds his bat behind the popping crease. Run-outs can come from direct throws at the stumps or when the ball is thrown to a team-mate who is near the stumps so that he can complete the run-out.

MAD FACT

Pakistan batsman, Inzamam-Ul-Haq was out hit wicket (see opposite) in a Test match versus England. He is also one of only three ODI batsmen to be out obstructing the field.

Caught

A player is out caught if the ball comes off his bat or his gloves below the wrist if either is in contact with the bat handle, and is caught before it touches the ground. Some catches involve the umpire deciding if the ball hit the edge of the bat or if the fielder's hands were underneath the ball before it touched the ground. If the player making the catch is the bowler, then it is out, caught and bowled.

West Indian all-rounder Dwayne Bravo takes an acrobatic one-handed catch.

Bowled and Stumped

To be bowled, the ball has to leave the bowler's hand and hit the stumps, dislodging the bails so that one or both fall off the stumps. There have been instances where the ball has nudged the wickets but the bails have stayed in place. In these cases, the batsman is not out. If a batsman hits the ball on to his stumps by mistake and the bails fall, he is still out bowled but is described as having played on. A player is stumped if he leaves his crease to play a shot, misses, and the wicketkeeper collects the ball and knocks the bails off while the batsman is out of his crease.

LBW

The leg before wicket (lbw) law is one of cricket's most complex rules. In simple terms, a player is out if the umpire believes the ball has pitched (bounced) in line with the stumps and would have gone on to hit them had it not been stopped by hitting the batsman's pads or any part of his body. A player can also be out if the ball pitches outside his off-stump but would have gone on to hit the stumps and the batsman made no attempt at a shot. He cannot be out if the ball hits his bat before his pads or pitches outside his leg-stump.

The shaded area is in line between the two sets of stumps. The red arrow shows the ball pitching in line and hitting the batsman's pads before the bat. As it would have gone on to hit the stumps, the batsman can be given out lbw. The purple arrow shows another ball that hits the pads first and would have gone on to hit the stumps. But because it pitched outside leg-stump, it is not given out.

Rare Dismissals

Five other ways of being out – hit wicket, timed out, handled ball, hitting the ball twice, and obstruction – occur very rarely. A batsman is out hit wicket when he dislodges the bails off the stumps with his foot, body or bat often by stepping back too far. Timed out, when the new batsman fails to walk out to the crease in a set time, has never happened at Test level. Only a handful of Test batsmen have been out handled the ball, the last to be so was England's Michael Vaughan in 2001.

PEOPLE ON THE PITCH

Cricket is played on an oval-shaped, grass-covered ground with its boundaries, the edge of the playing surface, marked out by ropes, triangular pads or fences. Situated in the middle of the ground is the pitch. This 20.12-m-long, 3-m-wide strip is where most of the game's action occurs.

Field Placings

A fielding team is made up of a bowler who bowls from one end of the pitch, a wicketkeeper who stands behind the stumps at the other end from the bowler, and nine fielders. The captain decides where these players should stand so that they are in the best position to stop runs and take catches.

Some fielders are placed close to the batsman. Slips, for example, stand to the side of the wicketkeeper and are in place to catch a ball that clips the edge of the bat. Other fielders are placed further away – for example, a third man is placed close to the boundary to collect the ball from shots that have eluded the slips. Point and cover are often busy positions with a lot of balls coming to them, so these are often the positions where a side's best fielders are found.

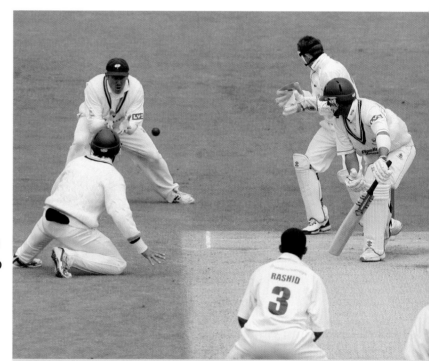

Anthony McGrath standing at first slip prepares to take a catch off the bowling of Adil Rashid during a 2007 County Championship match.

The range and names of fielding positions can seem bewildering, but the following pointers may help: deep or long tends to mean further away from the pitch and closer to the boundary; silly or short means the opposite. The entire ground can be split in two by an imaginary line running down the middle of the pitch. The half to the side of the batsman's legs is known as the leg-side or on-side. The other half is known as the off-side.

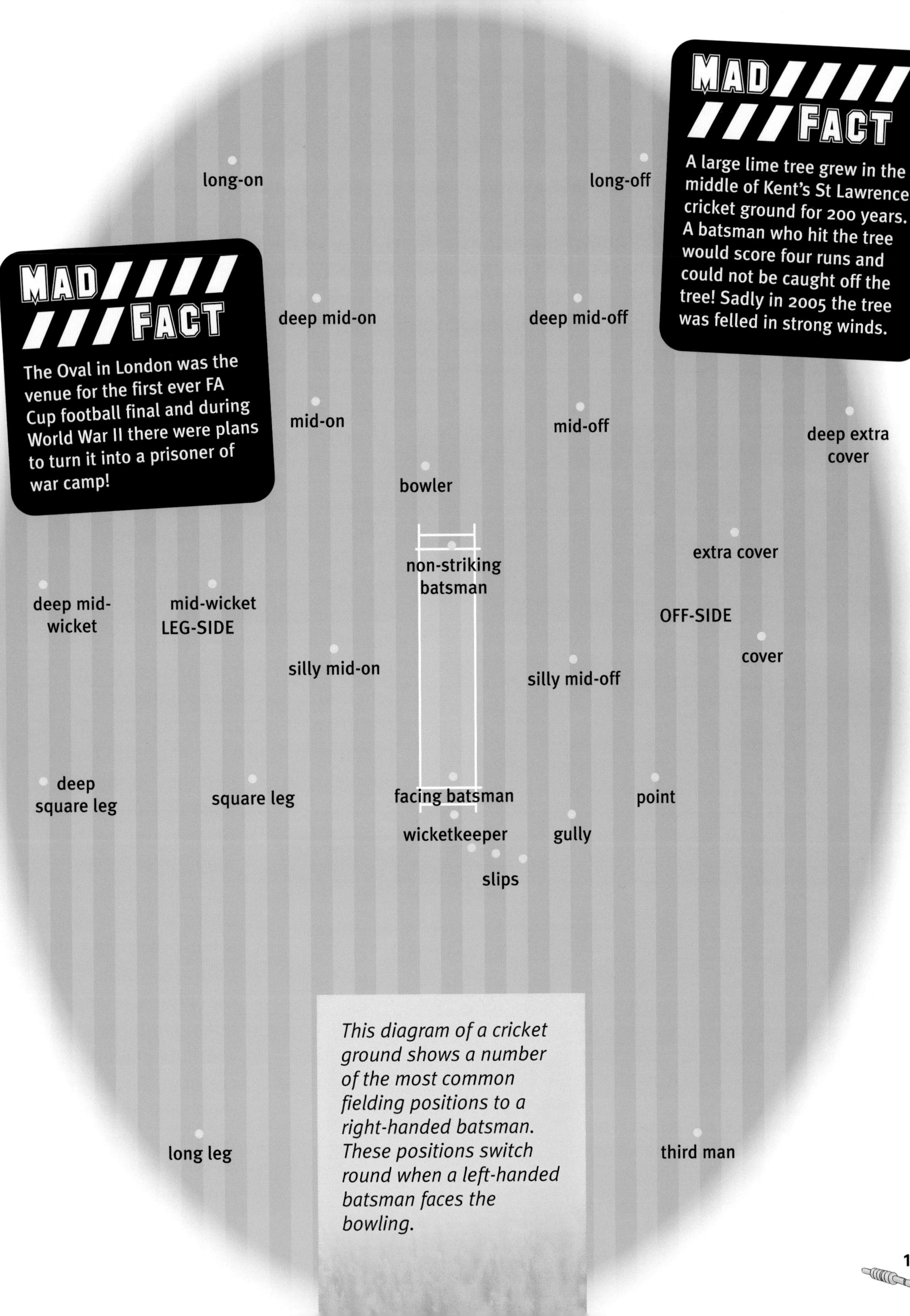

long-on
long-off
deep mid-on
deep mid-off
mid-on
mid-off
deep extra cover
bowler
non-striking batsman
extra cover
deep mid-wicket
mid-wicket
LEG-SIDE
OFF-SIDE
silly mid-on
silly mid-off
cover
deep square leg
square leg
facing batsman
point
wicketkeeper
gully
slips
long leg
third man

MAD FACT

A large lime tree grew in the middle of Kent's St Lawrence cricket ground for 200 years. A batsman who hit the tree would score four runs and could not be caught off the tree! Sadly in 2005 the tree was felled in strong winds.

MAD FACT

The Oval in London was the venue for the first ever FA Cup football final and during World War II there were plans to turn it into a prisoner of war camp!

This diagram of a cricket ground shows a number of the most common fielding positions to a right-handed batsman. These positions switch round when a left-handed batsman faces the bowling.

UMPIRES

Two umpires run a cricket match. One umpire stands behind the stumps at the bowler's end (also known as the non-striker's end) from where he has a direct view of the ball reaching the batsman. The other umpire usually stands at square leg. This gives the umpires a good view of the game in general and a particularly good view of potential run-outs or stumpings. After each over, the umpires swap positions.

New Zealand's Daniel Vettori celebrates as umpire Aleem Dar gives a batsman out. Top umpires are appointed by the ICC with ten umpires forming the elite panel for Tests and leading ODIs.

Umpiring Decisions

One of the umpires' main roles is to determine whether a batsman is out when a fielding team appeals. Umpires need a keen eye and concentration to determine, for example, whether a ball carried to a catcher or whether a batsman should be given out lbw. Umpires also judge whether a run scored goes to a batsman or is a bye or leg-bye. In all of these instances, the umpire has a special signal (see page 15) that he uses to communicate his decision to the players, spectators and the match scorers. For example, a leg-bye is signalled by the umpire touching a raised knee. Umpires also monitor players' conduct. Sometimes, they may have to warn a player, such as when a bowler repeatedly bowls dangerous deliveries.

STAT ATTACK

Most Test Appearances by an Umpire

119 S Bucknor (W Indies)

92 D Shepherd (England)

84 R Koertzen (South Africa)

76 D Hair (Australia)

73 S Venkataraghavan (India)

66 H Bird (England)/ D Harper (Australia)

Examining Conditions

Umpires are also responsible for deciding whether light and weather conditions are suitable for a game to continue. If conditions become especially gloomy, the umpires may offer the batsmen the light, meaning that the batsmen can decide whether to come off early. When players are called off for bad light or because of rain, umpires will continue to examine the pitch and the overall conditions to determine when the game can be restarted.

Other Officials

The increase in televised sport has put even more pressure on umpires to make the right decisions. A third umpire off the pitch has been introduced into top class games. If an umpire is unsure about a catch, a run-out or whether a four or six was scored, he can refer the matter to the third umpire by making a box-like signal with his hands. The third umpire watches television replays from different angles before reporting back to the umpires on the pitch. A fourth umpire looks after the other three umpires as well as the match balls. The match referee can discipline players for behaving badly and fine them or even ban them from future games.

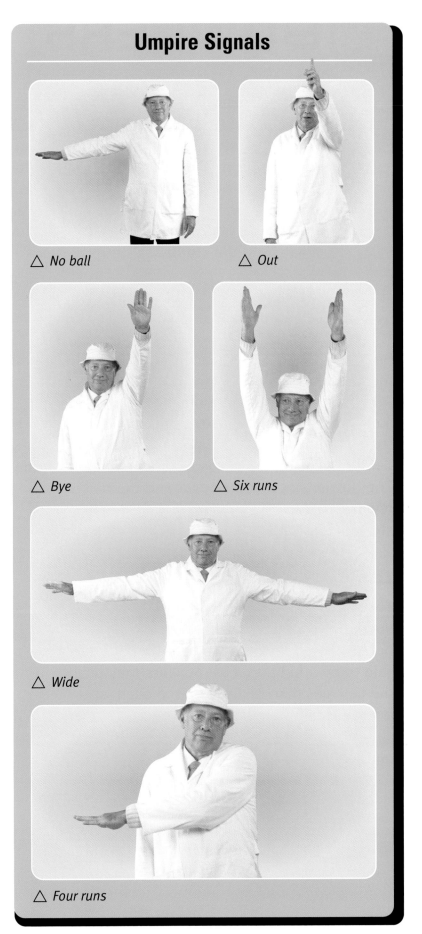

Umpire Signals

△ No ball
△ Out
△ Bye
△ Six runs
△ Wide
△ Four runs

BOWLERS

A bowler usually bowls a series of overs, known as a spell, from one end of the pitch. He has to inform the umpire which side of the stumps he plans to bowl from and can change this in between deliveries. Bowlers bowl either over the wicket, where their bowling arm is closer to the stumps, or around the wicket, where their bowling arm is further away from the stumps.

Bowling

Bowlers can be grouped according the speed at which they bowl – fast, fast-medium, medium or slow. A bowler marks out his run-up, which may be a couple of paces for a slow spin bowler or a 30m sprint for a fast bowler. The last step of the bowler's run-up before releasing the ball is called the delivery stride. The bowler's arm comes over and the ball is released before the bowler takes further steps to follow-through.

Length

The length of a delivery is judged by how far up the pitch the ball lands. If it does not hit the pitch before being struck by the batsman, then it is said to be a full toss. Fast bowlers may pitch the ball less than halfway up the pitch, at bouncer length, to send the ball rising up sharply into the batsman's ribs or flying past his head.

This diagram shows the approximate different lengths of a bowler's delivery. These will vary a little depending on the pitch and the pace of a bowler. A good length is a ball that makes a batsman unsure whether to go forward or back to play it.

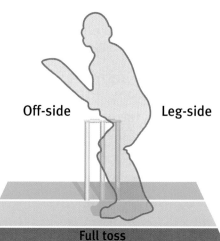

Off-side · Leg-side

Full toss
Full length/Half volley
Good length
Short of a length
Long hop/Bouncer

Wides and No-Balls

Bowlers work hard to avoid bowling wides and no-balls. A wide occurs when the umpire judges that the ball bowled is too wide or high for the batsman to reach with a normal stroke. A no-ball can be signalled by the umpire for many different reasons. For example, if the ball bounces twice before reaching the batsman or if the umpire believes the bowler is bowling dangerously or illegally. A no-ball is most often called when, in his delivery stride, the bowler's front foot oversteps the popping crease (see page 8) or his back foot steps on to the return crease. When a wide or no-ball is signalled, one run is added to the batting team's score and the ball has to be bowled again. In addition, a batsman can hit runs off a no-ball knowing that they can only be run out from a no-ball, not caught, bowled or lbw.

Who is...

...Muttiah Muralitharan?

Muttiah Muralitharan is a hugely successful Sri Lankan spin bowler. 'Murali' has already taken over 680 Test wickets and loves to bowl long spells in which he teases and tricks batsmen with his variety of deliveries. He is the only player to have taken ten wickets in a Test match against every other Test side. Born with a bent arm, his bowling action has caused controversy on a number of occasions, but he remains a popular figure with cricket fans all over the world.

Muralitharan comes in to bowl during an ODI. The Sri Lankan spinner has more than 450 ODI wickets.

BATSMEN

The batsmen's job is to score runs. They can do this only if they manage to stay in and avoid losing their wicket. This means that they have to mix attack and defence throughout their innings. Batsmen stand usually with their feet either side of the popping crease, with their heads up and eyes focused on the ball as it leaves the bowler's hand. The bat is gripped in both hands and taken back – the back lift – before they play a shot.

MAD //// //// FACT

Jason Gillespie came in as a night-watchman (see opposite) for Australia against Bangladesh in a 2006 Test. He went on to score an incredible 201 not out!

Different Strokes

Batsmen look to hit the ball in different ways depending on the line, length and speed of the bowler's delivery. The large number of different strokes or shots they play can be divided up in three ways – whether the ball is hit to the leg or off-side, whether they are attacking or defensive shots, and whether they are made with the batsman stepping back into his crease (back-foot shots) or moving forward (front-foot shots).

A short, fast delivery may force a batsman on to his back foot. From that position, he may play a backward defensive shot, playing the ball down safely in front of him. Alternatively, and if the ball rises high enough, he may choose to attack and swivel his body and bat around to play a powerful hook shot, sending the ball flying to the leg-side boundary.

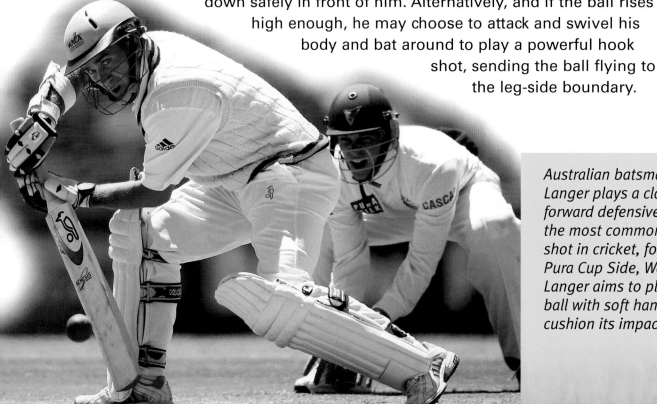

Australian batsman, Justin Langer plays a classic forward defensive, arguably the most common batting shot in cricket, for his Pura Cup Side, Warriors. Langer aims to play the ball with soft hands to cushion its impact.

Batting Order

The batting order of a typical team starts with the pair of opening batsmen. Their role in Tests and first class matches is to see off the new ball when it is at its hardest and fastest, and the opposing team is often at its most aggressive. It is not all about defence, though. Some superb opening batsmen, such as Australia's Matthew Hayden, see their role as more attacking and score heavily from the start.

A team's most stylish and often most effective run scorers are in the middle order – usually positions 3, 4, 5 and 6. These are the batsmen most expected to score a lot of runs, including centuries (100 runs). The wicketkeeper and bowlers who can bat well come next, with the side's least capable batsmen, known as the tail-enders, filling the last positions in the batting order. Sometimes, when a team loses a wicket near the end of the day, a more capable tail-ender goes in ahead of better batsmen to protect them. This player, known as a night-watchman, aims to see out the day's play.

South African batsman, Jacques Kallis, watches the ball race to the boundary.

STAT ATTACK

All-Time Leading Test Run Scorers (* means not out)

Player	Team	Matches	Runs	Highest Score
Brian Lara	West Indies	131	11,953	400*
Allan Border	Australia	156	11,174	205
Sachin Tendulkar	India	135	11,150	248*
Steve Waugh	Australia	168	10,927	200
Sunil Gavaskar	India	125	10,122	236*
Rahul Dravid	India	107	9,492	270
Ricky Ponting	Australia	110	9,368	257
Graham Gooch	England	118	8,900	333
Jacques Kallis	South Africa	107	8,851	189*
Javed Miandad	Pakistan	124	8,832	280*
Inzamam-ul-Haq	Pakistan	120	8,830	329
Viv Richards	West Indies	121	8,540	291
Alec Stewart	England	133	8,463	190

ALL-ROUNDERS AND WICKETKEEPERS

Squeezing enough good batsmen and bowlers into a side is often a headache for a team's selectors. What can make the task easier is the presence of a high-quality wicketkeeper who can bat well, and one or more all-rounders capable of batting and bowling to a high standard.

Who is...

...Andrew Flintoff?

Andrew 'Freddie' Flintoff is a powerful all-rounder for Lancashire and England. Flintoff is known for his impressive quick bowling, excellent fielding and, at times, brutal batting. He starred in England's 2005 Ashes victory over Australia. His 402 runs and 24 wickets tell only part of the story, as Flintoff was in truly inspirational form. He was named player of the series against India the following winter. Injury problems have restricted his career but he remains one of England's most extraordinary cricketers and has already notched up over 3,400 Test runs and over 200 Test wickets.

All-Rounders

Many batsmen are able to bowl a few competitive overs and all bowlers are expected to work hard on their batting. Some players, though, have the ability to bowl and bat with almost equally high ability. One of the greatest examples was the West Indian legend, Sir Garfield Sobers. He took over 235 wickets and scored 8,032 runs in Tests.

The 1970s and 1980s saw some of the best all-rounders, including India's Kapil Dev, Pakistan's Imran Khan, England's Ian Botham and New Zealand's Richard Hadlee. Today, the world's best all-rounders

Andrew Flintoff swipes a boundary while Australian captain, Ricky Ponting, looks on during the 2005 Ashes series.

include Andrew Flintoff and the South African pair, Jacques Kallis and Shaun Pollock. Such players are highly-prized as they have the potential to influence the game enormously with both bat and ball.

Wicketkeepers

Wicketkeepers are crucial to fielding sides. They stand behind the stumps and aim to field cleanly every delivery that passes the batsman, to prevent runs. They are often in prime position to catch a ball that nicks the edge of the bat or that is skied straight up in the air. Keepers stand back some distance from the stumps for fast bowlers, but 'stand up' to the stumps for spinners and some medium-pace bowlers. When close to the stumps, they are on the lookout for a stumping when a batsman lurches out of his crease.

Wicketkeepers require superb concentration and stamina to stop runs, take chances and field tidily throughout the day. They also need lightning reactions to make split-second catches and to spot and take run-out and stumping chances. At international level, wicketkeepers are expected to be decent batsmen as well as capable of scoring late-order runs. Some keepers, such as Adam Gilchrist (see page 37) are superb batsmen in their own right.

MAD FACT

Andrew Flintoff holds the record for the most sixes scored for England in Test matches, beating Ian Botham's record of 67. He has over 77 sixes and 457 fours to his total.

TECHNIQUES AND TACTICS

A major part of the fascination with cricket is the complex and subtle tactics and techniques used during a match by both sides. As the player in charge of a team's tactics, top captains, such as New Zealand's Stephen Fleming, England's Michael Vaughan and Australia's Ricky Ponting, analyze every move in a game to try to get ahead of the opposition.

Changing Conditions

Tactics vary based on the strengths and weaknesses of a team and its opposition, on how the game is going and on the weather conditions. Overcast skies can help swing bowlers and may prompt a side to bowl first. The condition and type of pitch also have great influence on tactics. Although they are carefully prepared, pitches vary hugely in how they play. Some are flat and true and ideal for batting for long periods. Others may be hard, fast and bouncy, which suits pace bowlers, or they may contain cracks and roughed-up patches that may suit spin bowlers. Pitches wear and continue to change their nature throughout a match. This may also prompt a captain to change his tactics.

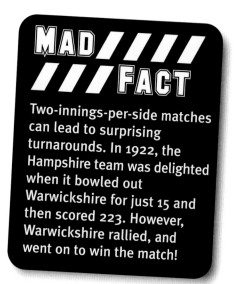

MAD FACT

Two-innings-per-side matches can lead to surprising turnarounds. In 1922, the Hampshire team was delighted when it bowled out Warwickshire for just 15 and then scored 223. However, Warwickshire rallied, and went on to win the match!

Australia set an incredibly attacking field during the 2001 Ashes series. Four slips and two gullies are in catching positions to the left of the wicketkeeper.

Captaincy

The captain can have a profound impact on a match. He may have a say in the selection of the team and will want to win the toss of a coin, which gives him the choice of bowling or batting first. Throughout a match, the fielding captain controls where he places his fielders and who gets to bowl and for how long. Different bowlers require different field placings. For example, a bowler moving the ball away from the edge of a batsman's bat at high speed might see more slip fielders brought in. As a game progresses, the fielding team may switch repeatedly between different tactics, attacking when they can, defending when necessary, but all the time on the lookout for wickets. If a wicket falls, a captain often moves more fielders into close catching positions to put pressure on the new batsman.

Long-serving New Zealand captain, Stephen Fleming has captained his side in 195 ODIs, more than any other captain. An astute and selfless leader, Fleming declared while on 274 not out against Sri Lanka in 2003, putting his team's chances of winning ahead of his own chances of making 300 and personal glory.

Declarations and the Follow-On

The captain of a batting side has fewer decisions to make, but these can also be crucial. He may change his side's batting order by putting in a night-watchman or moving a dangerous hitter further up the order to score some quick runs. If a team builds a large score, the captain may make a declaration. This means that his side's innings is over even though it has wickets to spare. The aim is to move the match on so that there is time to bowl out the opposition. A Test match side batting first that scores at least 200 runs more than the opposition in its first innings can choose to enforce the follow-on, making the opponents bat a second time in a row.

STAT ATTACK

Most Test Matches as Captain

93 Allan Border (Australia)

80 Stephen Fleming (New Zealand)

74 Clive Lloyd (West Indies)

57 Steve Waugh (Australia)

56 Arjuna Ranatunga (Sri Lanka)

FAST AND MEDIUM BOWLING

A team tends to go into a match with three or more bowlers who bowl at a medium, medium-fast or fast pace. These bowlers try to take wickets using pace, bounce, movement off the pitch or through the air, and variations in the deliveries they bowl.

MAD FACT

The fastest delivery officially recorded was bowled by Shoaib Akhtar of Pakistan in the 2003 World Cup. It was clocked at a rapid 161.3km/h.

Out and Out Pace

Used often in short, sharp spells including opening the bowling with the new ball, genuine fast bowlers such as Allan Donald, Malcolm Marshall, Shoaib Akhtar and Shaun Tait can be major match-winners. Given a helpful fast pitch, pace bowlers can sometimes terrorize batsmen, giving them little time to react, and generating lots of bounce into the batsman's body. Fast bowlers add to their threat if they are able to alter their length and pace to produce effective bouncers and slower balls.

Movement Off the Seam

Seam bowlers try to grip and bowl the ball 'seam up' so that the raised seam hits the pitch, making the ball move off the seam. If the ball hits a crack in the pitch, it may deviate sharply. Much of the time, seam bowlers aim to bowl a line around or just outside off-stump hoping to get a ball to nip back and hit the stumps or to nip away and catch the edge of the bat. They may bowl a delivery with the seam not up to slow the ball's flight or to create a different response off the pitch. Seam bowlers may also vary their line and length in an attempt to deceive a batsman and hopefully get him out.

Fiery South African pace bowler, Allan Donald, exhibits a powerful follow-through.

Swing Bowling

Swing is when the ball moves sideways through the air. Weather conditions and the position of the ball's seam can influence swing, as can polishing one side of the ball while keeping the other side rough. Away or out-swing is when the ball curves to the left through the air, from the bowler's perspective. In-swing is when it curves to the right. Swing can be devastating, but also hard to control. Some bowlers are better at generating one type of swing than the other. When the ball is swinging through the air, bowlers tend to bowl a fuller length to give the ball as much time as possible to swing in the air before pitching. Reverse swing is a phenomenon that sees an old ball swing in an opposite direction to the one expected. It seems to work mainly when bowling fast, as Simon Jones proved in the 2005 Ashes Series.

Who is...

...Glenn McGrath?

Never blessed with express pace, Glenn McGrath became one of the world's greatest seam bowlers through his incredible accuracy, skill and massive will to win. Making his Test debut for Australia in 1993, McGrath's probing accuracy with the ball saw him take 563 Test wickets at a very low average of 21.64 runs per wicket.

In 2004, when many people thought he was past his best, he proved them wrong with an incredible 8 for 24 against Pakistan – his best ever figures. McGrath also took 381 ODI wickets and finished leading wicket-taker at the 2007 World Cup, after which he retired.

This four stage sequence shows Glenn McGrath leaping into his delivery stride, bringing his arm over and releasing the ball.

SPIN BOWLING

Spin bowlers pose batsmen quite different problems from pace bowlers. While batsmen can deal with the slower speed (usually 70–90km/h) of the ball, they have to contend with the unpredictable flight, bounce and sideways movement, known as turn, from a spin bowler's delivery.

Off-spin Bowling

Off-spin or off-break bowling sees the ball spun with the fingers to move it from left to right off the pitch. Off-spin bowlers may also make use of an arm ball – a delivery that looks the same as their off-break, but does not spin, instead it continues straight. A small number of off-spinners, such as Muttiah Muralitharan, have perfected the doosra. This devastating delivery spins the opposite way to an off-break. A left arm off-spinner, such as England's Monty Panesar or New Zealand's Daniel Vettori, poses different problems to a batsman, as his basic ball spins from right to left across a right-handed batsman.

Monty Panesar broke into the England team in 2006 and has become a firm favourite with fans. He took six wickets in an innings in the 2007 First Test against West Indies on a pitch at Lords not particularly suited to spin bowling.

STAT ATTACK

All-Time Leading Test Bowlers

Bowler	Team	Wickets	Average
Shane Warne	(Australia)	708	25.41
Muttiah Muralitharan	(Sri Lanka)	700	21.73
Anil Kumble	(India)	566	28.65
Glenn McGrath	(Australia)	563	21.64
Courtney Walsh	(West Indies)	519	24.44
Kapil Dev	(India)	434	29.64
Richard Hadlee	(New Zealand)	431	22.29
Shaun Pollock	(South Africa)	416	23.19
Wasim Akram	(Pakistan)	414	23.62
Curtley Ambrose	(West Indies)	405	20.99
Ian Botham	(England)	383	28.40
Malcolm Marshall	(West Indies)	376	20.94

Shane Warne is the greatest leg-spin bowler in the history of the game. His Test debut in 1992 saw him concede 228 runs for 1 wicket but he went on to terrorize batsmen, taking an incredible 708 Test wickets. Warne single-handedly boosted spin bowling's popularity all over the world with his amazing deliveries and many match-winning performances. He also became a dangerous lower-order batsman scoring 3,154 Test runs. Although he never made a century, he once reached 99. He retired from international cricket after Australia's 5–0 Ashes series win in 2006/07.

Leg-spin Bowling

Leg-spin or leg-break bowling was an almost forgotten art at cricket's top level until the emergence of players such as Abdul Qadir in the 1980s and Shane Warne in the 1990s. Leg-spin bowling sees the ball spun with a sharp wrist action so that it spins from right to left. A good leg-spin delivery may pitch on or around a right-handed batsman's leg-stump but turn to hit off-stump. Leg-spinners cannot get a batsman out lbw if their deliveries pitch outside leg-stump. Top leg-spinners have devastating variations in their armoury. The googly, which is bowled out of the back of the hand, spins the opposite way to the leg-break, while the top spinner is a ball that does not spin sideways but instead hurries straight on to the batsman.

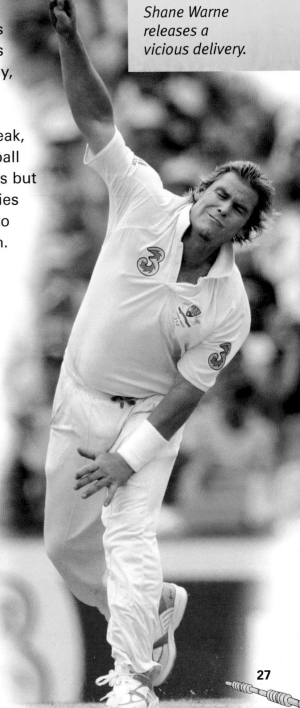

Shane Warne releases a vicious delivery.

MAD FACT

Throughout his career, Shane Warne has bowled 40,705 balls in Tests, 10,642 balls in ODIs and over 73,500 balls in first class matches.

Flight and Guile

Putting spin on the ball is only part of a spin bowler's armoury. Spin bowlers need terrific accuracy to pitch the ball again and again in spots where the batsmen are forced to play. Many spinners, especially on unhelpful pitches, vary their flight and line slightly, trying to tempt batsmen into a rash stroke. Successful spinners also need a calm temperament; they must always be thinking of how to get batsmen out and must not allow an assault on their bowling to affect them.

KEEPING IT TIGHT

The fielding side is always on the hunt for wickets, but there are many occasions where keeping the game tight and preventing heavy run scoring can prove vital. Thoughtful field placings and good bowling and fielding that repeatedly stop singles and boundaries not only keep the score low; they can also lift a player's own team and frustrate the opposition's batsmen into a mistake that might lead to a wicket.

Drying Up Runs

Captains constantly tinker with their field placings in an effort to stop batsmen scoring. With most bowlers bowling a line on or just outside off-stump, a 6-3 field with three fielders on the leg-side and six on the off-side is common. The six off-side fielders may be found in the slips or in singles-saving positions or close to the boundary. Sharp fielding, when allied to tight, accurate bowling can lead to a series of maiden overs with no runs scored. This really puts the pressure on the batsmen.

Fielding Techniques

In the past, fielding was considered a secondary activity to bowling and batting, but the rise of limited overs games has changed that. All players now need to be expert and athletic fielders. When fielding a low ball, players try to get their whole body behind the ball to create a

STAT ATTACK

Most Test Match Catches

181	Mark Waugh (Australia)
164	Brian Lara (West Indies)
159	Stephen Fleming (New Zealand)
157	Mark Taylor (Australia)
156	Allan Border (Australia)
147	Rahul Dravid (India)
125	Shane Warne (Australia)
124	Ricky Ponting (Australia)
122	Greg Chappell (Australia)
122	Viv Richards (West Indies)

New Zealand's Lou Vincent performs a sliding stop to field the ball.

www.nzcricket.c

long barrier in case the ball bobbles over their hands. When chasing a ball heading for the boundary, fielders sometimes make a slide stop, flying across the ground to halt the ball before it or they touch the boundary rope.

Most Dismissals by a Wicketkeeper

Total	Player	Caught	Stumped
402	Mark Boucher (South Africa)	383	19
395	Ian Healy (Australia)	366	29
381	Adam Gilchrist (Australia)	344	37
355	Rodney Marsh (Australia)	343	12
270	Jeffrey Dujon (West Indies)	265	5

Throwing In

Stopping the ball is only half the story. Players must send the ball back to a team-mate close to one set of stumps, usually at the wicketkeeper's end, with a flat, accurate throw. When a fielder sees a batsman well out of his crease, he may throw to that end, aiming for the stumps to cause a run-out. A bowler or another fielder should be backing up (standing close to the stumps) ready to field the ball if it does not hit the stumps directly. Poor backing up or a wild throw can lead to additional runs, known as overthrows, being scored.

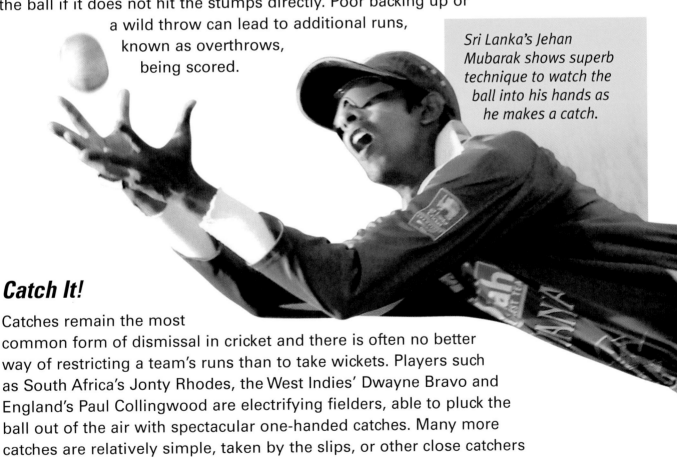

Sri Lanka's Jehan Mubarak shows superb technique to watch the ball into his hands as he makes a catch.

Catch It!

Catches remain the most common form of dismissal in cricket and there is often no better way of restricting a team's runs than to take wickets. Players such as South Africa's Jonty Rhodes, the West Indies' Dwayne Bravo and England's Paul Collingwood are electrifying fielders, able to pluck the ball out of the air with spectacular one-handed catches. Many more catches are relatively simple, taken by the slips, or other close catchers at waist or knee height, or by fielders taking high catches out near the boundary. When catching, players try to watch the ball right into their hands, which they bring back into their body to cushion the ball's impact.

All batsmen have their favourite strokes to play, from a thumping drive to a delicate nudge or push shot. A major part of top-quality batting is to perfect a large range of strokes to deal with different deliveries in attack and defence.

Michael Vaughan practises the sweep shot in the nets. This is an attacking stroke played against spin bowlers when the ball is pitched outside of leg-stump. The ball is swept behind and to the leg-side. All batsmen hone their game through hours of practice in the nets.

MAD //// //// FACT

Kumar Sangakkara and Mahela Jayawardene came together with Sir Lanka at 14 for 2 in the 2006 First Test against South Africa. When they were separated, the score had moved on to an incredible 638! Jayawardene made 374 and Sangakkara 287, a world record partnership.

Scoring Singles

Batsmen can sometimes adjust certain strokes used mainly for defence so that they score singles from them. For example, the forward defensive can be adjusted with the face of the bat angled slightly to one side to nudge or push the ball into gaps. The backwards defensive stroke can be turned into a run-scoring shot by swinging down on the ball and punching through with a firm bottom hand. If there is no close leg-side fielder, some players are good at playing a delicate leg glance. Here, they deflect a ball down and around on the leg-side for runs.

Putting Away the Bad Ball

Batsmen have to be patient, especially against high-quality bowling. They are always on the lookout for a poorly directed, 'bad' ball, from which they try to score. A ball bowled short and wide of off-stump, for example, can be played with the bat almost at arm's length to perform a powerful cut stroke. With a cut shot, batsmen aim to roll their wrists to hit the ball down to avoid being caught. A short ball that does not get up as much as the bowler intended, can be hit aggressively on the leg-side using a pull shot. Balls pitched up can sometimes be hit on the half volley (just as the ball

bounces on the pitch) using the drive shot. The lofted drive is an aggressive stroke that is played mainly against slower bowlers and when fielders are close in rather than out towards the boundary. The ball is played up and over close fielders and heads towards the boundary.

Taking Runs

As soon as a batsman has played a shot, he should be ready to run. His batting partner, on the edge of his own batting crease as the bowler bowls, will have advanced several paces up the pitch and will be in a good position to complete a run or get back into his crease if he or his partner calls "no". Quick running between the wickets has several benefits. It can see singles stolen and can turn singles into two runs and twos into threes. It also rotates the strike, meaning that the other batsman will face the next ball.

The drive is one of the most common scoring shots in cricket. It is played on the front foot. An off-drive sends the ball into the off-side, while this straight drive by Australia's Patrice Berthold sends the ball back down the ground past the bowler and often to the boundary.

BUILDING AN INNINGS

No batsman wants to be out for a duck (without scoring) but it takes patience, determination and calmness under pressure to build a big innings. Batsmen also need to choose the right shot to play at the right time to stay in the game.

Play or Leave

When first coming in to bat, batsmen have to be extremely wary and must judge the conditions of the pitch and how the bowlers are bowling. They try to play themselves in, concentrating on defence early on until they feel they have the measure of the pitch and the bowling attack. Throughout their innings, batsmen have to decide whether to play a shot or leave it and let it go through to the wicketkeeper. Patience is key even in hectic limited overs games.

Who is...

...Sachin Tendulkar?

Sachin Tendulkar is a master batsman who announced his arrival in first class cricket with a century on his debut at the age of 15. The following year he made his Test debut for India and has since scored over 11,000 runs, including 37 centuries in Tests. A brilliant innings builder, Tendulkar has been just as successful in One Day Internationals, where he has amassed over 14,800 runs and some 50 man-of-the-match awards. Tendulkar is considered one of the finest batsmen ever to play.

Sachin Tendulkar is perfectly balanced as he looks to hit a delivery during an ODI against England.

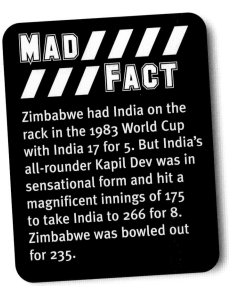
Pacing an Innings

Individual batsmen and whole teams have to pace their innings according to the conditions. They may be scoring freely until a new bowler comes on or a number of their team-mates lose their wickets – events that may force them to defend more. They may target a weaker bowler to score a lot of quick runs off or, if batting with a poor tail-ender, may try to keep themselves facing the bowling as much as possible. Batting in limited overs games can pose different challenges. The first team to bat has to judge what is a good score on the pitch, while the second team chases its target knowing the run rate (the number of runs per over required) and feeling the pressure if the rate starts to climb.

Tail-end Batting

Tail-enders try their hardest to support a recognized batsman who is still in, defending their wicket and trying to get the batsman on strike to face as many balls as possible. The runs made by the last three or four batsmen in a team can often make the difference between success and failure. In 2006, for example, Pakistan had slumped to 39 for 6 against India before a century from Kamran Akmal and 45 runs each from Shoaib Akhtar and Abdul Razzaq took them to 245, helping them to win the Test.

STAT ATTACK

Highest Test Match Innings

952-6 dec	Sri Lanka v India	1997
903-7 dec	England v Australia	1938
849	England v West Indies	1929/30
790-3 dec	West Indies v Pakistan	1957/58
758-8 dec	Australia v West Indies	1954/55
756-5 dec	Sri Lanka v South Africa	2006
751-5 dec	West Indies v England	2003/04
747	West Indies v South Africa	2004/05
735-6 dec	Australia v Zimbabwe	2003/04
729-6 dec	Australia v England	1930

Pakistan's Younis Khan plays a backward defensive against a rising ball during the World Cup. He makes sure he gets on top of the ball to direct it downwards to avoid giving away a catch.

THE BIG COMPETITIONS

Cricket can be played in different ways, from short matches for amateurs played in the evening to five-day Test matches for the world's best players. Test matches, One Day Internationals, including the World Cup and first class cricket are seen as the top competitions, but limited overs matches between states, counties or provinces have proved very popular with spectators.

Domestic Limited Overs

Limited overs cricket was first played at top level by English counties in 1962. It quickly became popular and now every major cricketing country has at least one, and often several different limited overs competitions between states, provinces or, in the case of the West Indies, islands. Most competitions are now 50 overs per side, just like ODIs, but some competitions are not standard length. These include the 45 overs-a-side Standard Bank Cup in South Africa, which is competed for by six teams, and the 40 overs-a-side Pro 40 competition which features 19 teams – the 18 English counties plus Scotland.

Four members of the 2005 World XI one day team – Kumar Sangakkara, Daniel Vettori, Shaun Pollock and Kevin Pietersen.

Who is...

...Karen Rolton?

Karen Rolton is the Australian women's captain who has excelled in all forms of the game. A powerful batter, she is Australia's leading woman Test run scorer, has the highest score made in a women's Test match of 209 not out, and has over 3,900 runs in ODIs. She also holds the Twenty20 record for the highest score made in an international, when she scored 96 off of just 53 balls against England in 2005. In 2006, she won the first ever ICC Female Player of the Year award.

Left-handed batswoman, Karen Rolton plays a pull shot during a Test match versus England. Rolton has a Test batting average of 66.

Twenty20

Most club cricketers who play for fun are familiar with 20 or 30 overs-per-side games fitted into an evening or afternoon. Twenty overs-per-side matches for professional players were first introduced in 2003 in Britain. Known as Twenty20, they have been such a hit with crowds that national teams began playing them in 2005. The first ever ICC Twenty20 World Cup was played in South Africa in 2007 and was won by India.

With so little time, the emphasis in Twenty20 is on attack and taking risks to score boundaries. Exciting stroke play is encouraged, with fielding restrictions that include five fielders required to be inside a 30-yard (about 27-m) circle marked on the pitch for the whole innings, and eight fielders inside the circle for the first six overs. The highest international score so far is 221 for 5 by Australia in 2007.

MAD //// //// FACT

In a 2002 C&G Trophy limited overs game, Surrey's Alistair Brown blitzed an incredible 268, a world record score in limited overs cricket. An amazing 192 of his runs came in boundaries – 30 fours and 12 sixes.

ONE DAY INTERNATIONALS

The first One Day International came about by chance. Rain had washed out the Test match between Australia and England in Melbourne in 1971, so a one day game was played with 40 eight-ball overs per side. Since that time, ODIs have developed rapidly with their own rules and competitions.

Rules and Restrictions

ODIs are now played over 50 regular six-ball overs per side, with teams in colourful clothing rather than whites. Each bowler can bowl a maximum of ten overs, or a fifth of his team's overs if the number is cut back because of the weather. Restrictions on where fielders can stand have been tinkered with to help run scoring. In 2005, powerplays arrived. These force the fielding team to place only two fielders outside a 30-yard circle surrounding the pitch for 20 overs of an innings. The first 10 overs of an innings are always a powerplay. The fielding captain then has to choose two blocks of five overs to be the other powerplays.

This sequence shows Herschelle Gibbs becoming the first batsman to strike six sixes in an over in One Day Internationals. He achieved this in the 2007 World Cup against the Netherlands.

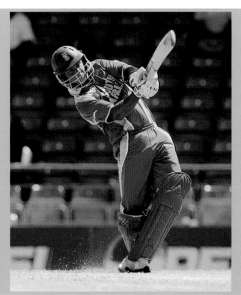
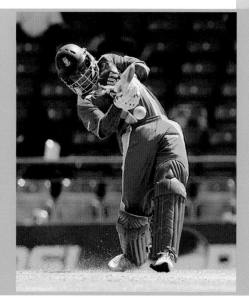

A Game of Runs

While some matches are won by bowling the opposition out, the emphasis in ODIs is on scoring and preventing runs. Batting tactics can involve using an aggressive batsman, known as a pinch hitter, to score boundaries at the start of the innings or playing carefully to conserve wickets before launching an all-out assault in the last ten or so overs. With good conditions, ODIs have increasingly become a run-feast for top batsmen. The highest ever score in an ODI between two top nations was posted by Australia in 2006 against South Africa – 434 in 50 overs. Astonishingly, South Africa managed to exceed that in the same game, scoring 438 and winning the match.

ODI Competitions

Over 2,600 ODIs have now been played in a variety of competitions. Teams that play Test matches against one another, often play a series of ODIs before or after the Test series. Sometimes a third team is invited to form a triangular tournament. The ICC Champions Trophy occurs every two years and features all the Test playing nations. Women's cricket has had a World Cup for ODI matches since 1973. Two years later, the first men's World Cup was staged in England and won by the West Indies. Since then, the World Cup has been held approximately every four years, with Australia winning three in a row in 1999, 2003 and 2007.

Who is...

...Adam Gilchrist

Adam Gilchrist is a hugely exciting and entertaining Australian wicketkeeper and batsman. He has notched over 5,300 runs in Tests, while his aggressive stroke play has seen him amass over 9,000 ODI runs. Gilchrist can score at a devastatingly quick rate as witnessed in 2006, when he battered the second fastest ever Test century in just 57 balls. His exhilarating 149 in the 2007 World Cup final guided Australia to victory.

MAD FACT

In a 2001/02 ODI versus Zimbabwe, Sri Lanka's Chaminda Vaas recorded extraordinary bowling figures of 8 for 19 – the best in any ODI.

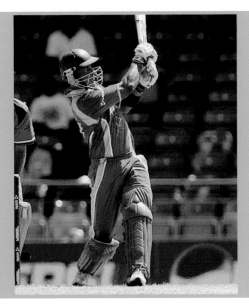

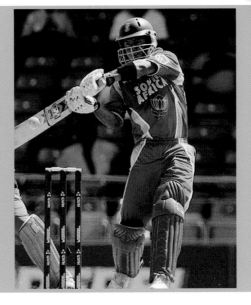

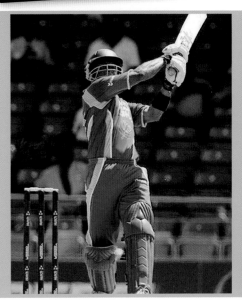

FIRST CLASS CRICKET

First class cricket is the highest level of cricket played within a country (its domestic cricket). Matches tend to be two-innings-per-side games, usually lasting for three or more days.

Major Competitions

All Test match-playing countries have first class competitions, from New Zealand's State Championship (formerly the Shell Trophy) to Pakistan's Qaid-i-Azam Trophy. In South Africa, the Supersport Series (formerly known as the Currie Cup) features 11 teams divided into two pools. Each team plays the others once. The top three teams in each pool move on to a Super Six stage to determine the teams that will contest the final. In India, the Ranji Trophy sees 15 teams compete in two groups in its Super League. These include Mumbai, the competition's most successful side, which has 37 titles.

Sourav Ganguly (left) runs between the wickets during a Ranji Trophy match for his side, Bengal, the runners-up in the 2006/07 competition.

County Cricket

First class cricket in Britain is played by 18 county sides from England and Wales (Glamorgan). In 1992, Durham became the first county in 71 years to be admitted to the championship. Games are up to four days long with the winners gaining 14 points. A draw is worth four points and a bonus-point system rewards successful bowling or batting in the first innings. For example, a team scoring over 400 runs within the first 130 overs of its innings gains four bonus points. In 2000, the championship was split into two divisions with relegation and promotion between them. This has added an edge to many matches and has seen shocks, such as the 2005 champions, Nottinghamshire, relegated the next season.

STAT ATTACK

Recent County Championship Winners

2007	Sussex
2006	Sussex
2005	Nottinghamshire
2004	Warwickshire
2003	Sussex
2002	Surrey
2001	Yorkshire
2000	Surrey
1999	Surrey
1998	Leicestershire

Pura Cup

The Sheffield Shield was launched in the 1890s and was renamed the Pura Cup at the end of the twentieth century. The Pura Cup pits Australia's state teams against one another. Different formats have been used. The 2006/07 season saw each of the six state sides play each other twice, once at home and once away. Points are awarded not just for wins, but also for which side scores the most runs in their first innings. At the end of the competition, the top two point-scoring sides meet in a one-game final held at the top point scorer's ground. The onus is on the second-placed side to win the game because a draw sees the top side win the competition. 2006/07 proved a landmark season in the Pura Cup with the newest side to the competition, Tasmania, which joined in 1982/83, winning the championship for the first time.

Other Matches

Certain games which are not part of a country's top national championship are also given first class status. These include games between England's Oxford and Cambridge universities and matches involving the Australia 'A' side. When a major national team tours another country it usually plays Test matches and some other matches against local first class sides. These are also counted as first class games.

STAT ATTACK

Recent Sheffield Shield/Pura Cup Winners

2006/07	Tasmania
2005/06	Queensland
2004/05	New South Wales
2003/04	Victoria
2002/03	New South Wales
2001/02	Queensland
2000/01	Queensland
1999/00	Queensland
1998/99	Western Australia
1997/98	Western Australia

Yorkshire's Michael Vaughan is run out by Nick Pothas of Hampshire during a 2007 County Championship game. The Championship has lured many top overseas players, including Shane Warne.

TEST CRICKET

One Day Internationals may be popular with crowds, but Test match cricket, with its two-innings-per-side format, is still considered the peak of the game. It is the ultimate cricket competition where the best players in world cricket most want to prove themselves.

STAT ATTACK

First Test Match per Country

England	1877
Australia	1877
South Africa	1889
West Indies	1928
New Zealand	1930
India	1932
Pakistan	1952
Sri Lanka	1982
Zimbabwe	1992
Bangladesh	2000

Test History

The first official Test match was played at the Melbourne Cricket Ground (MCG) in 1877. Australia beat England by 45 runs, but England rallied to win the second Test by four wickets. Since that time, almost 2,000 Test matches have been played between teams from ten Test playing nations (see Stat Attack). These are often three, four or five match series between two sides where the teams compete for a trophy. For example, since 1996, the Border-Gavaskar Trophy series has been played between Australia and India. Since 1963, the Wisden Trophy has been played for by England and the West Indies. In 2001, the ICC began a Test Championship system where each side aims to play the others over a six year period. The results then feed into a league table based on success. The top three teams in 2007 were Australia, England and Pakistan.

The Australian Test team appeals to umpire Billy Doctrove while playing South Africa.

Five Day Strain

In the past, a number of Test matches were timeless. This meant that they lasted however many days it took both teams to complete their two innings. The last timeless Test in 1939 saw the game abandoned as a draw after the tenth day. England was on 654 for 5, chasing a target of 696, but had to leave South Africa to catch their boat home! Today, a Test match lasts a maximum of five days with a minimum of six hours' play each day, often at a level of intensity far higher than domestic cricket. Bowlers usually bowl dozens of overs at peak performance, batsmen may bat for eight hours or more, and a team may be in the field for two days if its opponents amass a big total. Those players who succeed are not only talented, but are also able to cope with the pressure of playing for their country against the best opponents in front of large, passionate crowds.

MAD //// //// FACT

England's Wilfred Rhodes recorded the longest Test career of any cricketer, 30 years and 315 days. He was 52 when he played his last Test match.

Who is...

...Vivian Richards?

Nicknamed the Master Blaster, Sir Viv Richards was a swashbuckling batsman who struck fear into his opponents with his forceful and often brilliant batting. In 1976, a year after helping West Indies win the first World Cup, Richards struck a phenomenal 1,710 runs in just 11 Test matches at an average of 90.00. Ten years later, he hit the fastest ever Test century off just 56 balls. An excellent fielder, whether in the slips or prowling the covers, Richards ended his Test career with 8,540 runs.

The majestic Viv Richards in action sending the ball rocketing to the boundary.

Women's Test Cricket

The first women's Test match was played in 1934 between England and Australia. Since then, the two sides have gone on to contest 15 series against each other, with Australia leading six to three with six drawn. The female sides of all the male Test playing nations, except for Bangladesh, have joined these two teams. In July 2007, the tenth women's team with Test status, the Netherlands, played its first ever Test match against South Africa.

THE ASHES

The most famous Test match series in the world is the Ashes. It is the oldest Test series – it started in 1882– and is played between England and Australia. The series gets its name from a small urn said to contain the ashes of the bails burned to celebrate Australia's 1882 defeat of England.

Incredible Performances

Today, held over five matches, the Ashes is a massive event on the cricketing calendar and reputations are often made or broken during the series. In 1930, for example, the great Sir Donald Bradman (see page 44) scored 300 runs in a day as Australia triumphed. Three years later, England concocted a plan, known as Bodyline, where they bowled aggressively at the batsmen not the stumps. They may have won the series, but they made few friends. The 1938 series was remembered for a record 903 for 7 innings by England, with Sir Len Hutton scoring 364, leading to the biggest winning margin in Test history – an innings and 579 runs. In 1956, England's spinner, Jim Laker, took 19 of the 20 Australian wickets for just 90 runs, a record that still stands. The 1970s and 1980s saw a glut of truly great cricketers, from Dennis Lillee to Graham Gooch battle it out for Ashes supremacy. In 1981, incredible heroics by Ian Botham managed to turn likely defeat into a stirring series victory. 1993 saw the arrival of Shane Warne. During that series, he bowled what many people call 'the ball of the century'. It landed outside leg-stump, turned wickedly, so much so that it clipped Mike Gatting's off-stump on the way to an Australian series triumph.

Who is...

...Ian Botham?

Sir Ian Botham was an electrifying all-rounder for England, capable of match-winning performances with the bat, ball and in the field where he was superb and took 120 Test cricket catches. He pummelled 5,200 Test runs with the bat and took 383 Test wickets. A boisterous character, Botham was rarely out of the news for either his on or off-pitch antics throughout his long career for England, three English counties (Somerset, Worcestershire and Durham) and Queensland, Australia. A tireless charity worker, Botham was knighted in 2007.

Ian Botham roars in to bowl during an Ashes Test.

The Australian team celebrates its 2006/07 success with captain, Ricky Ponting, holding a replica of the Ashes urn.

Australian Dominance

There have been 316 Ashes Tests; 131 have been won by Australia, 97 by England and 88 have been drawn. The gap between the two sides' wins has increased since the 1986/87 series. Australia has dominated and won all apart from one of the series since then. The exception was in 2005, when England won an enthralling and exceptionally close contest, with the Edgbaston Test won by just two runs, the smallest margin in Ashes history. Despite England suffering a 5–0 whitewash in the 2006/07 series, interest remains enormous for the next series in 2009.

TEST CRICKET LEGENDS

The sport of cricket has generated hundreds of notable players. Here are five of the finest to have played Test match cricket.

Sir Donald Bradman

'The Don' is remembered as the greatest batsman of all time and his statistics back up this claim with ease. In just 52 Test matches for Australia between 1928 and 1948, he scored 29 centuries and made an astonishing 6,996 runs. In a game where the best batsmen have batting averages in the high forties and fifties, Bradman's record Test average was a staggering 99.94. He needed only four runs in his very last Test innings in 1948 to retire with an average of 100, but was out without scoring. It was a rare failure by a man whose highest score in Tests was 334 and, in first class cricket, 452 not out.

Brian Lara

Brian Lara was an extraordinary West Indian batsman who amassed a record 11,953 Test runs and 10,453 ODI runs during his career.

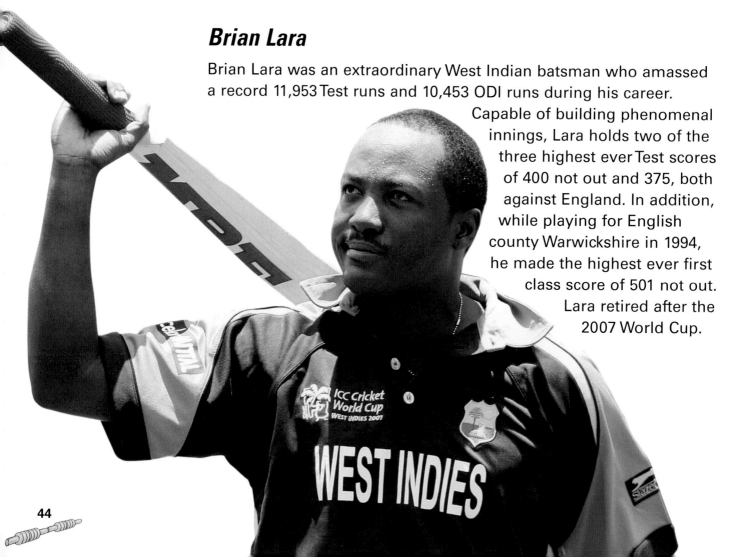

Capable of building phenomenal innings, Lara holds two of the three highest ever Test scores of 400 not out and 375, both against England. In addition, while playing for English county Warwickshire in 1994, he made the highest ever first class score of 501 not out. Lara retired after the 2007 World Cup.

Imran Khan

Pakistan's Imran Khan was one of the greatest all-rounders to grace the game. He was an exceptional and hostile fast bowler who took 362 Test wickets. He was also a powerful middle or late-order batsman who scored 3,807 Test runs and 3,709 runs in One Day Internationals. As captain of his country, he marshalled Pakistan to many memorable wins, including winning the 1992 World Cup.

Malcolm Marshall

Malcolm Marshall was the shortest of the fearsome West Indian fast bowlers of the 1970s and 1980s, but he was arguably the most devastating, too. Bravery, great pace and a brilliant cricket mind helped him to reach 376 Test wickets, including an awesome 7 for 53 in 1984 against England when bowling with his left hand and broken thumb in plaster. A hugely popular cricketer, Marshall was only 41 years old when he died tragically of cancer.

Kapil Dev

The best ever Indian all-rounder, Kapil Dev was a superb, pacey right-arm bowler who mastered swing bowling to take 434 Test wickets in 131 Test matches. He made his debut for India in 1978 and quickly proved himself to be an aggressive batsman who thrilled spectators by often taking the attack to the opposition. His last Test was against New Zealand in 1994, by which time he had scored 5,248 Test runs.

GLOSSARY

All-rounder A player who is almost equally skilled as a batsman and a bowler.

Average (batting) The number of runs scored in a career or season divided by the number of innings in which the batsman was out.

Average (bowling) The number of runs scored off a bowler's overs divided by the number of wickets he has taken.

Backing up A fielder who gets behind the stumps to prevent overthrows when fielding.

Bouncer A short-pitched ball, which passes the batsman at chest or head height.

Boundary The edge of a cricket field. It is also used to describe a batsman scoring a four or a six.

Bye A run scored when the batsman does not touch the ball with either his bat or his body.

Caught and bowled When the bowler catches the batsman out off his own bowling.

Century When a batsman scores 100 or more runs in an innings. A half-century is a score of 50 or more and a double century is 200 or more runs.

Declaration When a team chooses to end its innings before all of its wickets were lost. In scoring, the abbreviation *dec* is used to note a total after a declaration.

Delivery The word used to describe a ball bowled at the batsman by a bowler.

Duck When a batsman is out without having scored. If he is out on the first ball without scoring, it is called a golden duck.

Extras A word used to describe all runs scored without the bat, such as no-balls, byes and wides.

Flight The path of the ball through the air when it is bowled.

Hat-trick When three wickets are taken with consecutive balls by a bowler.

Maiden over When a bowler completes an over without giving away any runs.

Non-striker The batsman who is not facing the bowling.

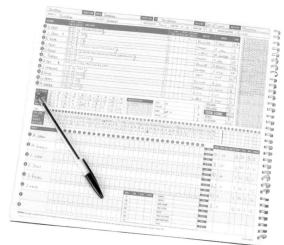

ODIs One Day Internationals which, today, are 50 overs-per-side matches played between national teams.

Over A series of six legal deliveries bowled by a bowler from one end of the pitch.

Overthrows Runs scored when the ball is thrown in towards the stumps but not cleanly fielded.

Return crease The markings that run at 90 degrees to the bowling and popping creases.

Selectors The people who choose the players for a team.

Stamina The ability to maintain physical effort over long periods.

Stock ball The basic delivery a bowler bowls regularly.

True pitch A pitch that has even bounce and thus is easier to bat on.

Twelfth man An extra player allowed to field, but not bat or bowl, if a team-mate is injured.

Umpires The officials who control a cricket match and make key decisions on whether a player is out or not and whether runs have been scored.

Wide A ball which bounces so high or lands so wide of the stumps that it is very difficult for a batsman to reach it.

WEBSITES

WWW.CRICINFO.COM
A terrific website for cricket lovers with statistics, records, news and profiles on every international cricket side and details and scorecards of every single Test match and major One Day Internationals.

WWWW.CRICKET.COM.AU/
The official website of Cricket Australia is packed with features and information on state, national and international cricket.

WWW.ECB.CO.UK/KIDS/
A section of the English Cricket Board website devoted to cricket for children and teenagers. The site includes games and details of initiatives for younger players including Kwik Cricket, Inter Cricket and Urban Cricket.

WWW.CRICKETWEB.NET/COACHING/INDEX.PHP
A large section of the excellent cricketweb website is devoted to tips and explanations of key batting, bowling and fielding techniques. Also check out the huge collection of links to other cricket websites.

HTTP///3LIB.UKONLINE.CO.UK/CRICKET/INDEX.HTML
This website has short videos of legendary players in action, from Ian Botham and Allan Donald to Viv Richards and Dennis Lillee.

Note to parents and teachers:

Every effort has been made by the publishers to ensure that these websites are suitable for children, that they are of the highest educational value, and that they contain no inappropriate or offensive material. However, because of the nature of the Internet, it is impossible to guarantee that the contents of these sites will not be altered. We strongly advise that Internet access is supervised by a responsible adult.

INDEX